Steinbert's Method

By
Leah Baugh

Illustrated by Jeni Tomlinson

WestBow Press books may be ordered through booksellers or by contacting:

WestBow Press
A Division of Thomas Nelson & Zondervan
1663 Liberty Drive
Bloomington, IN 47403
www.westbowpress.com
1 (866) 928-1240

Because of the dynamic nature of the Internet, any web addresses or links contained in this book may have changed since publication and may no longer be valid. The views expressed in this work are solely those of the author and do not necessarily reflect the views of the publisher, and the publisher hereby disclaims any responsibility for them.

Any people depicted in stock imagery provided by Thinkstock are models, and such images are being used for illustrative purposes only. Certain stock imagery © Thinkstock.

ISBN: 978-1-4908-7766-2 (sc)
ISBN: 978-1-4908-7767-9 (e)

Library of Congress Control Number: 2015906428

Print information available on the last page.

WestBow Press rev. date: 04/24/2015

WestBow®
PRESS
A DIVISION OF THOMAS NELSON
& ZONDERVAN

To Grace Noelle
My great inspiration

Steinbert
saw a bird...

up in the sky.

Then, he had a
QUESTION

What could it be...

...that makes the bird
FLY?

So, he watched and **OBSERVED** it

and **SAW** what it did,

But, that wasn't enough
to uncover what
was hid.

Then, he tested and tested,

EXPERIMENTED, *too!*

Until, he figured out how the bird flew.

As the bird was flying 'round and 'round,

Steinbert decided to write it all down...so, he **RECORDED** the **DATA** of what he had found.

At last, making a **STATEMENT** **CONCLUSION** and all, he told everyone why the bird didn't fall.

So, if you see something and want to know how it's done...

1. Question
2. Observe
3. Test
4. Write
5. Share

...use Steinbert's method he knows it's the ONE!

First, when you see it,
make your best guess.

A HYPOTHESIS,
a THOUGHT,
an Idea!
that's the best.

Then, do your homework, prepare for a test, **EXPERIMENT** many times 'cause you're on a quest!

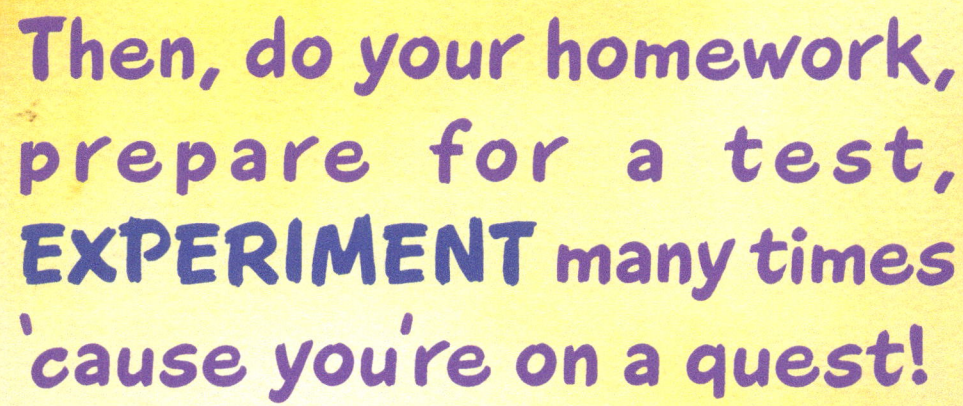

Next, **RECORD** what you find...to remember the rest.
COMPARE and **CONTRAST**...

ANALYZE it all...Keep right on going...
don't drop the ball.